The Helen Poems

The Helen Poems

Victor Depta

Ion Books
P.O. Box 111327
Memphis, TN 38111-1327

Ion Books
P.O. Box 111327
Memphis, Tennessee 38111-1327

Library of Congress Cataloging-in-Publication Data

Depta, Victor.
    The Helen poems / Victor Depta.
       p.   cm.
    ISBN 0-938507-22-2 : $12.95
    1. Fathers and daughters--Poetry.   I. Title.
    PS3554.E64H44   1994
    811' .54--dc20   94-29365
                                                 CIP

Acknowledgements

Grateful acknowledgement is made to the editors of the following publications in which these poems have appeared:

Aura: "Genesis II"
Black Fly Review: "Worrywart"
Calliope: "Daughter Flower" and "The Dance Recital"
Crosscurrents: "The Litigation"
Grasslands Review: "Flute Lessons"
Kansas Quarterly: "Genteel Dad"
Memphis State Review: "A History of the Western World" (published as "Unruly Boy")
New Mexico Humanities Review: "The Siege of Twilight" (published as
        "Resurrection")
Nightsun: "Poem Father"
Outerbridge: "Band Supper" and "Driving Lessons"
Panhandler: "The Girl-Lady" and "Sorry, My Mistake"
Riverrun: "Wise Father" and "I Forgot That"
Soundings East: "The Generations of Long Distance"
South Carolina Review: "Fix the Bike"
West Branch: "The Immigrant Generations" (published as "Translations")

Cover illustration by Helen Depta, a drawing at age six
Book design by David Spicer

CONTENTS

I

II

III

IV

I

Amtrak Song

I sighed as the train came, and yet why
when already a continent was between us.
What could a thousand do, in miles, and how adjust
which we hadn't done, and out of goodbye
we had wrung all grief long ago
and parting was a dry afterthought on the platform
in the January wind, and the snow.
The child was in my arms, and you were leaving.
The Panama Limited stopped with its giant eye
its great blue arrow and silvery cars.
The conductor waved you forward into your dreams–
the noise, the steps, the glamorous windows–
while the child leaned, weeping, clutching at your sleeve.

The Litigation

Like a white chastisement
your small letters come
and I'm astonished they contain so much
I have to open again–
parcels of accusation, rebuke and blame
the cartons of remorse, torn packaging
and in the smallest boxes, carefully wrapped
is the grief I open last.

Daughter Flower

I would never have believed
the child could ease me out of myself
no longer young, divorced and aimlessly bereaved
and inclined to weep

frequently wanting to die
knowing how little hope there was
spendthrift as it longed to rise
like weeds in the empty lot

the groundsels, mustard and field daisies
but futile, and I was close to tears
so when she pointed to the violets along the fence
I saw that perseverance in the coming years

like the flowers which she knelt to
the leaves and blossoms in her small, white fist
would be enough, and a gentleness came upon me
which was my duty, and resembled bliss.

Chauffeur

Conversion to the flesh
child-fresh
burden of sweet bones
and if they fell away
faith-melt, I
in a tumbling free fall beyond Saturn–
suited, helmeted–would spiral toward the stars

so I'm careful with the kids
sit down, stay put
when they pile in back of the truck
back under the shell
when, like a ponderous goose
and a trailing fuzzball line of chicks
we in our glory go
honking and waddle-slow
to the city pool.

The Immigrant Generations

I inherited, as a few gold coins, my grandmother's vowels
her rich, blurred references to Joseph, the good King
to Prague, and to faraway Nicholas.
She sighed for her old country
her Catholic soul at a loss in the Appalachians
where folks said *pooched* and *hooved*
heared and *cheer*, and *I've wearied myself nigh death.*

The newsreels brought us history on film
the recent horrors of the past on flimsy celluloid
where fact and entertainment flared to nightmares in the
        movie house
while above the mountains the clouds passed
above us in the coal fields
where the sun never shines

and education, how like a burnt house
charred, skeletal–sparks, ashes in the wind
night glow, blue flames in our bewilderment
and yet, it seemed, the poets left their dedications
also, to me

when they gazed on the visions in their books
puzzling at the mystery which admits no foolishness from us
the living, no blurring of grief or joy
and their labor I often overheard
ambiguously sweet, or like a rasp on stone
my brother and sister, my prosody.

I've got my beer-joint diction
my flaky atmans, funky bodhisattvas, juke box tales
my evicted language on the streets
oh fuck, and all such truck
while every second thought's immured in a threat of fire—
my plates and cups, my house near the cotton fields—
and a child, drowsy at being read to
who hears her father lapse into golden vowels
the sweetest consonants in her history
and yawns, so sleepy.

The Chandelier and the Moon

I've been converted
to wrinkled hands in the dishwater
to a polish-cloth, its hands and knees on the floor
to a paint brush and brilliant white
at the casings

where I sigh
being so poetic at the windows
which are darkened by the dining room chandelier
at midnight, as I peer out at the moon
that paints the grass in a great swath
eerily gray, silvered with dew

which transforms me
as a hierodule in a temple
while the train whistles far away, a dog howls
a shadow on the lawn becomes a cat–
a father, pleased to submit and serve

because he can look now, while she sleeps
at his dark image in the panes without a shudder
and he can finish–the paint lid pounded on
the thinner, the clean brush–
and witness for the white surrender.

The Dance Recital

For my daughter
what choice was there of a dance teacher
our being so far from New York, Paris, Moscow
but to settle, Midwest, for a munchkin
en pointe, from Munich
for civilization thin as the jet exhausts
high over the Mississippi–
it was silly, anyway, my friends' encomiums for her
pathetic frauds–*Why, she could have been*
and so forth.

My daughter was beautiful, nonetheless
at five, still blond, unblemished, fair
her eye-color delft, cornflower
her costume pink sateen, with pink slippers
and in the blue, theatrical lights–
the clouds on the backdrops like clumsy cherubs–
her arms outstretched, and on tiptoe for the bow
she ran to me
but halted, in her error, at the proscenium
as angels do.

Babysitters

The babysitters
so *other* she's exposed to
the girls from the Christian Center
what do they do? watch soft porn
nymphomaniacs, pyromania in the kitchen
child molester, plying her flesh.

They probably play Rook, Crazy Eights
read to her Rumpelstiltskin
the boy whose nose grew
Jiminy Cricket
pop popcorn
but I'm not sure what they do

while I'm on the road
rubber banded, making ends meet
squinting in the headlights after night class
worried–
they're so like MTV
Cheeze Puffs, Beef Jerky.

Guilt-Forgot

You were reading
homework-child on the couch
and I
it was gaze-nothing, stare-thought
yet I was face-fraught
I must have been
so frown-wrung
for you to have come to me
and ask
Did I do something wrong, Daddy?

The Fourth

Partying at the lake, the State Park
no booze, firecrackers, sparklers
on the Fourth of July–
we did it anyway
me and my buddies
drunk, delirious as cicadas in sex-lust
death-dangerous as the bacchants
Orpheus in the firelight

and my daughter cried
No, Daddy, it's against the law
and suddenly
descended as eye-glasses
a focus on a small face in the dark
white, peering up
No, Daddy!
panicked as Eurydice.

Next to the Graveyard

My house
my little territory
graveyard bordered
headstone-quaint on the south
highwayed, neighbored
also

there, in the drive
branch-leafy, water-cries
we wash the truck
my daughter-help paid for (bribed, really)
her slapdash, a fun help
soapy, rag-palm, slant fountain of hose.

It is an idyll, two innocents in the leaf glow
though she is the sweet one
child-blond, thin, fair
my idol hose-happy, spraying me, joy shock
gold emerald on the grass, and the leaves
breeze-glittering.

The Celibate

I was so cool
as she stood by the boy
hair tassel silk, eyes-blue
flesh pale-pure and frail, her seven years
and him, Chicago tough, the eight year old
the frown in his forehead
crease, sweet danger there, already
definitely displaced in the south
flipping through *Penthouse* at my kitchen table
while I washed dishes

so cool
I found it, he said
pillow-fallen, legs spread
sure you did, sure your father did
breast-burdened–
I glanced at the oily sheen, thighs, abdomen
splayed flesh, the vivid fingernails at the cleft–
and I let them look, so cool
my daughter, the female
the boy
and perfect parent.

Lent

I holler at my daughter
come look at the clouds
or *come look at the wild viola*
the spring beauties, out here on the lawn!
but it doesn't help much, self-conscious
like an awkward first line of a poem.

She calls to me nowadays
come look at the birds
or *come look at the squirrel*
hurry!
and I dutifully go to the door, the window
and peer at the crape myrtle, the pecan tree.

I'm so busy, usually
that I glance and record
irises blue-furled, the azaleas salmon-pink.
I do so while starting the truck
and go on without a sigh
a lyric or a psalm.

Spaghetti Supper

When the garlic bread fell from the tray
and Miss Caterpillar screamed *Child, be careful!*
I nearly fainted
thinking she meant me.

God, a spaghetti supper–
dingy pastel, plastic chairs, long tables–
children should riot, hold Caterpillar hostage to pasta
demand meatballs, negotiate salads.

My daughter is so polite
I wonder she doesn't strangle
explaining to my neighbors where her mommy is
between mouthfuls, proud and humiliated.

I hate it when they pity her
the drunks, the adulterers, the Valium freaks
who have every right to speak, since each has a spouse
each has a house so bored the stove yawns.

I hate it when they pity me
Why doesn't he marry, eligible as he is
I hear them whisper in their Coke cans
Why?
I swear to god, a grown man could cry.

Bath Time

It's awkward with a girl.
I have to say
Now wash your butt and butterfly.
I repeat that through the door
worried that she'll fall in the tub
that her ears are dirty
she won't wash between her toes

and when she comes out
damp-lovely in her robe
I get to comb, blow dry
trim her ragged nails.
I get to pamper and pet
caress, make over
sweet, downy, my daughter.

II

The Siege of Twilight

The distant armament
on the horizon where the clouds are trenched
explodes through the trees
and strikes my daughter playing on the lawn

though certainly no blood
when she's hit by the golden shrapnel
no contusion or scrape
no walls collapse on her loveliness.

She does not die.
I can stand in an Armageddon such as this
unknown to casualties
and call her name.

Worrywart

A frozen winter, I hate it
snow, ice storm, more snow
though the kids are in heaven
angels on the ground, snowballs, snowmen
and sled riding past dark.

I trudge to the hill to drag her home
but no, she needs a push, just one more
and one more, and one more.
I sigh, glance at the stars, and shove.

As she drops away I worry.
It's so dark down there
she goes so fast, out of my hands
so unseen in the white-dark, bluing-dark
her yells so distant.

I shudder and look at the stars.
God, I think, how literary, how symbolic
but, as a matter of fact, the night was starry
brilliant-hard, dark-glittering
and she slid away from me, many times.

In Day Care

Another month of snow–
surprised, again, the south closed its schools
and my girl was in day care, crowded
expensive among the children as I dropped her off
waiting till she got to the door
before I crunched away in my chains.

Early one day, in a blizzard
I went to gather her up
in the warm-humid, milk-ginger room
and found the children on pallets, refugees of cookies
and my daughter crooning to them
lullabies, *Hush, little baby, don't you cry.*

The director shushed me
and then in the kitchen, babbled about my girl
what a grown-up little helper she really was.
The woman made me nervous.
Authority usually does

and I wished
cowering from her strong-armed, coy prattle
that I was in the day room
on the pallet with cookie breath
drowsy, drifting to sleep
in my child's care.

The Movement

for Adrienne Rich and *The Dream of a
Common Language*

Women
often enough
I have heard you cry out
sympathetically
because I nursed an infant
a daughter, day after day
with a bottle
month after month
and I had wished for breasts
flat ones
like those of a cat or a dog
and small nipples
but I had dreamed of breasts, of milk
nevertheless.

Fix the Bike

Parents who say to kids
You stupid thing! Can't you do nothing?
are all wrong
since children will bleed, stone-hard
turnip-dry, a face like a pimple
and despise the dad father
whom they would love
obviously

so I was patient with her
fixing the flat tire, adjusting the brakes
but somehow, as with Sheba in Israel
the wrench ended up,
the screwdriver, the air pump, in my hands
while she murmured on the porch steps
bejeweled, in saffron and cerise
in glorious silk given over
to her womanish role.

Her Camping Trip

In the truck bed, in a sleeping bag
face skyward, oppressed by the humid stars
and skittering, mind flickering maws, dread cuniform
mitotic, fecund, horrible. I sat up in a panic
drank wine, smoked cigarettes

while my daughter slept.
At daybreak she stretched and yawned, said *good
        morning, daddy*
pulled on her sneakers and strode through the brush
stumble-butt, to her business, then washed her hands and face
pointing to the wisps of fog on the water.

And at the fire, after juice, milk, bread, boiled eggs
she fussed with her tackle box
and hurried to cast with her feathered flies.
I followed, sick to my stomach
and sat on the bank, trembling and sweating
trying to read a book. I glanced up, shocked
when she reeled in the lip-hooked, flexing bass.

She let them go, none big enough.
And hearty, in a wilderness mood
she cleaned the camp, aired the sleeping bags, gathered wood.
She had us tramp upstream and down.
We read in the afternoon, lolled about, ate hot dogs
and went to bathe, she lather and splash in her suit
while I, waist deep, turned to look at the hyssop

the water millet, the loosestrife and mallows at the
    water's edge
so peaceful in the fading sun–soft pink and bits of white
so blurred in the rippling glitter of evening–
that I would have wept but for the child
who wouldn't understand such tears
and would be frightened.

A History of the Western World

That daughter of mine, I took her comic books
(she wouldn't make her bed, hang up her clothes, put her
      toys away).
She fled to the lot out back, flung herself in the grass
and thrashed about, though when her fury eased
she lay in a nest (I'd like to think, as I spied from the
      kitchen)
and saw the kingdoms.

She saw the sweet pea at the corner of her eye–
how it curled on the sage
and over the millet made its way to the green goldenrod,
its tiny lobes of leaves in pairs, with ringlets and curlicues–
how it lay on the yarrow and the feverfew
and scooped the dew with violet cups
and served to bumblebees, all day,
a nectar that they staggered on
and lost their way.

She saw the thistle and the queen anne's lace,
who bristled with purple crowns,
who from their daises looked down
at the fillets on their slender gowns,
and frowned and frowned.

She saw, among the sumac and the sage,
the sprouts of locusts and mimosa trees,
which will–if the mower doesn't come, and all destroy–
as trees with towering fronds,
on spiky and on languorous limbs,
bring the weedy melee to an end

and she, forgetful of Superman and Thor,
curled in her nest among the nations–
the ripening purpletop and millet swaying–
and looked at the sky with half-shut eyes,
saw spangles of the sun, the rainbows flashing
on her eyelashes.

The Adult One

She seems so grown-up, so calm
while I flounder in my passions
death-passion, romantic-passion, sex-passion.
She does her math, watches Scoobie Doo.
She asks adult questions, like
Can you help me with these square roots?

I don't know what square roots are—
honest descendants, boring kin, turnips with four sides—
I don't know. I can't help her.
Oh, Dad, really!

What has happened to me? I must be mentally ill.
I laugh in the midst of a kiss, yet swoon for the might-be of
      a smile
dreaming for days, lowering the doorstep of my expectations
till there's nothing left but grass, a weedy path, a wildflower
ridiculous.

What's happened to me?
Every third step is a curb, every fourth a cliff.
I can't bear the sight of a mortuary. So windowless
no plate glass view of the finest model
no discount coffins propped on stands, no mannequin
      mourners.
They're bricked up, polite as a bank, those death prisons
as bad as a dead dog in the road, its red mass, bone-white,
      tongue-loll.

I'm frightened as Himalayas by any height
guard rail, banister, balustrade, which I fall from.
I am the play-dad, thespian daddy, desperate to do
and with a father like me, how can she be so calm—
I envy her—so much the adult one.

Girl Scouts

You in Girl Scout Camp–two weeks–
and me at the house
needful-weak
and in the attic-basement roam–
who to cook for
pretend fright-clutter to, in your room
so neat

and your return
peel-sunburn
long tangle-hair gnawed on and braces broke
poison ivy, ear infection
sneakers, backpack, mud, clumps of moss–
a sweet mess, room tromp through
and home.

The Generations of Long Distance

The old hurt too expensive to pay for again
when my ex-wife telephones
we're courteous, with nowhere to begin
but when my daughter comes on the line
to tell me she misses me–but she's ok
has been to Grandma and Grandpa's three times
has been to the beach, the ice rink on her summer visit–
my heart's made wealthy again.

An hour's not too much, a week, to pay for
but she rushes to her story's end
as if, across the continent, her life were a litany
which stopped
and I, with nothing but her breathing on the phone
know the distant god, the *father*
the one without a duty who grieves and asks
What else, honey?
What else you been doing?

Rescue Her

Rescue my child from the future
a helicopter, rope, a halter
iodine
blood, marrow
seat belts
stars in the windshield

save her from wind shear
malfunctions
derailment, the head-on
rescue her from the sex plague
rape

from a sac breath like L.A.
Chernobyls in every room
dead radio
light
heat
wind.

Ping-Pong

A book in my hands
a cosmos of horrors, in essays–
recombinant DNA, cyclotrons, dopamine, serotonin
methane on Jupiter, neutrinos, pre-adaptive traits–
all ghost stories, gory materialists skittering through my
        mind.

What's wrong, Dad? my daughter asks.
I tell her nothing's wrong, I was only reading.
You look so worried, she said.
I'm bored, Daddy. Why don't we play some Scrabble?
Ping-pong, maybe?

She wasn't bored
and I'm beholden in the basement
a paddle in my hand *ping-pong*
(echoic reduplication, I looked it up, really scary)
laughing and pleased to lose.

The Operation

It's not unusual I was calm.
An appendectomy is a clam bake
easy as falling off a log, and such like
so I bought a book, *Shogun*, or something
and settled in.

I wasn't prepared, mid-samurai.
No one told me
shifting her from the cot to the bed
that she'd thrash and strangle
I can't breathe! I can't breathe!
and stare bewildered, blank-eyed as a carp

or that, when she was quiet
her sweaty hairline damp as a seal's
she'd be told by a nurse
Even though your tummy's sore as the dickens
you'll have to cough
and you've got to sit up, darling, as much as possible.

So we sat up, more or less, for a day and a half.
Don't make me laugh, Daddy, she said. *It hurts.*
We watched TV.
We walked the silver pole down the corridor and back
the IV bag like a catfish on a hook.

No one had said a word.
No one told me that her sleep
that the anesthetist might
much deeper than Morpheus
drown her.

Flute Lessons

What rest is there
with a daughter in the dining room
her squeal-scales on the flute
like slaughtered pigs
I asked myself

but with a young man, a flautist I found
whose idol was Jean Rampal, to teach her
she blossomed Bach-wise
in the practice room at school
for his sweet discipline
so spine upright, flute straight, fingering, all that

so now I lie on the couch
wine-easy, divine as an emperor
played to
or Saul
eased in his soul
as she practices.

Winter Nights

Praise be to her
to Scrabble, to Trivial Pursuit
to wallowing on the couch in front of TV–
I wake up from them wondering where I've been
what sweet haven, Sharon, Lily

and ask, where did death go
what child has led me through the wilderness
to that, that Canaan of entertainment
to Password, picture puzzles
whose only point I know of
during all those hours
is oblivion, blessedness.

Band Supper

In the middle of America
or close to it, near the Mississippi
there's a band supper each fall
when we eat barbecue and coleslaw off styrofoam plates
with white bread and Coke

while the band thumps and squeaks in a martial discord—
the kids, my daughter along with the rest
in blouses and trousers, epaulets and chin straps
frumpy as a brass band in Yugoslavia.

It's understandable why we wince
why we squirm on the portable bleacher
why we gaze over their plumed box-hats
why we wish for concerts, symphonies
and that all squealing clarinets turned to lead.

I stared absently across the road
and my mind was suddenly filled with light
lost, momentarily, in what it saw—
the golden soybeans, the browning oaks.
They became rare, beautiful

and the power poles
the lighting fixture company
Wal-Mart and Highway 45
vanished while the band
pathetic and absurd, became a requiem.

III

The Brace-Face Kiss

My daughter, so sweet
so close to me, who sits on my lap
who sneaks a kiss, she confesses
on my mouth
tender, peach-wet
voluptuous as the flush, frail skin of a 12 year old
so puffy, fragile as a membrane

my brace-face
my giggling child
and oh, so blood wild for a moment
so devouring *one*
so to clasp her delicious
delirious in the pain-ease
the yoke-white of origins
and we, both of us, cease to be.

Good lord!
I'm about to croak
get yourself off me, I laugh
and after a week
blood-dead as Reason
offhand as a cat at calculus
I discuss incest.

The Girl-Lady

You want to go humpbacked?! I shouted.
You're going to look like a witch.
But I know why she stoops
why, in junior high
quick to develop, as she calls them, her boobies

she wears huge blouses
sweaters like sackcloth
giant coats
harassed as she is by thin-clumsy
inchoate boys

their awe-wonder, fear-longing
piping voices, cracking into bass
pestering her like feists at a lady's horse
queenly
baggy in her gown.

Father Moon

She broke a dish at the sink and wept suddenly–
petulant, despairing tears
and for a second I stood frightened
at the edge of a father's cliff.

I hate my body! she shouted.
I'd rather be a man.
And like rope burns, clumsy rappel, I asked
Is it your period?

It's the rag!
and she turned away
the demeaning, vulgar trash of the word
shaming her mind, she knew
and not the world-moon of her sex, her discomfort.
It's really a bitch, she sighed
toxic shock, mini-pads, Midol, all the crap.

That's true, I suppose
but if you were a man
you'd worry about getting it up.
I never thought of that, she said, wiping her eyes.

And you'd symbolize, you understand, for virility
motorcycles and TransAms
and strut your biceps like bird hackles–
you've seen those Nature films on PBS
the two bull moose, the walruses–
a lot of violence.

I guess you're right, she remarked
bored with my lecture, already.
*Men can't...*but the telephone rang mid-sentence
and she ran to answer it.
Men can't, I shouted
They can't have babies!

Self-Conscious Girl

I'm fat, my hair's all greasy, and I got pimples!
she wailed
though I knew better than to chuckle.
She would scream, *You never take me serious!*
and wall up, hostile as the Middle East

so I talk about the frog prince
the ugly duckling, the beauty-beast.
Yeah, they're all men! she shouts.
Sleeping beauty, then, I say
Cinderella, Rapunzel.
That's kids' stuff, she groans.

I want to say
Well, what about me, flesh-hanging
my shriveled chrysalis, death-butterfly
but sigh, instead
take out the Oxy-Wash, Noxzema
shampoo, the jogger's diet.

What She Reads

Seven hundred pages of science fantasy
science fiction, Gothic horrors
Dune, The Stand, Wolfsfane–
is that what I gave up TV for
me reading about the plutonium and hydrogen difference

kilotons and megatons
the electromagnetic pulse, fire ball, heat blast
radiation and nuclear winter–
all that, since I'm bored with fiction
and she reads fast food for the mind?

I left Dickens on the coffee table–
hint, hint–Cooper, Twain, Stevenson, Eliot, the Brontes
but no, not for her
so I watched PBS
Cosmos, Nova, Nature.

She watched, too, offhand, and remarked
We screw up everything, don't we, Dad?
and picked up her tome, her glitzy covered
mirrored, silver see-through
from Wal-Mart.

Cleaning Her Room

Child disaster room creep tentacles crustacean clutter
in the hall flotsam debris cast coat flung
shoes stepped out of leg-warmers kelp socks
sand in her room
her struggle to the bed
books piled like dunes
quilts in clouds
and collapse.
Don't bug me, Dad.
I need a nap.

The Grown-Up Miracle

A triangle
as in Egypt with Potiphar's wife
and so went my friends, like dead phones
a pyramid collapsing on a corpse, crushed gold
a mummy love, anyway
a five week silence

and my lady friend
reckless as Imperial Rome
sent message after message, couriers
ambassadors of fraud to my small kingdom
vodka-ridden, frightened, petty with fury

so, blind drunk
I dialed a dozen *fuck you's* on the phone
blind to my daughter, school-home
bewildered, scurrying her friends from the door
and out till midnight.

Therefore, at dawn
while she wept in the kitchen, I explained
I won't apologize for my anger.
Granted, otherwise, I was a scumbag
and I'm sorry.
You understand.
I won't apologize for my anger.

And lo, as if a miracle out of Egypt
a Constantine in Rome
when she smiled.

Breakfast Time

The odor of bacon, salt meat
strips sizzling brown, crunch vision as I lay in bed
wondering what in the hell?
and coffee, the flicker of a TV commercial in my mind–
white shirt, brown face and hands
the emeralded shrubs, a sack–
but the odor was actual, moist
pungent as the vacuum hiss from the can
luxuriant as Sunday.

Hey, Dad, it's breakfast!
and I leaped out of bed
wondering what possessed her, what whim.
I was charmed by her fussy commands
Now drink your coffee and then your juice
soothed by her play-house manner
her dominion, dictatorial with the plates, the silverware
and painful, suddenly, as the lack of a wife.

Homework

My daughter's fifteen
and reads with a Teddy Bear.
I noticed a girl, once, do the same on a flight from L.A.
I loathed the pilot
who teased, leering at her, as we deplaned–
the bastard.

So unself-conscious, my daughter
as she rests her cheek against the Bear's face
so sweetly limp on the couch
her physics textbook open against her ribs
the headphones for MTV awry at her temples.

She sighs and settles against the Bear
well into sleep, a thin line of spittle on her cheek
and I will have to wake her as gently as I can
so she won't startle *What? Huh?*
the Bear less than a pillow
as she drags it
sleep-drugged into bed.

Sex Talk

After breakfast, now, she needs her coffee
and from her fat, brown mug–it's never
never to be touched by a soul but her–
a childish rule for so adult a ritual
though I don't want her to use mine, either
I confess–the green-yellow dragon mug
gaudy trash, like a Chinese K-Mart.

For our weekend brunch, in the glow of the kitchen window
a light which helps, since I haul at meaning
a day laborer in the lost house of reality
and pile up warmth like forearms on a fence–
two jays, three sparrows and a mourning dove–
I fry the bacon, she the scrambled eggs

a week's catching up to do, mostly over coffee.
So, Nancy is pregnant
and you had to take her for the test!
Linda is crazy about Dale!?
You forgot your flute lesson, by the way.
Have you thought about a major?
Biophysics? What in the world is that?
I don't know, she says, *but it sounds good.*

How is it going with Charles?
About the same, she replies
though the walls of Troy might echo bitterness
as she withdraws from the towers.
Well, I always want what's best for you.
And Rome rises up in aqueducts
for the man on water skis
whom she loves.

Don't you get lonely, Dad? she asks.
You didn't go out Friday night, or Saturday.
I was going to reply
oh, maybe sometimes, a little
and I wanted to add
your boyfriend's an illiterate, white, hairless ape.
What do you do? she asks.
I mean, uh, do you go blind?

Wise Father

Because my life's pretty dull
and because her mysteries scare me
as if her face lacked parts
and our talks like an answering machine

I aggravate my daughter for details
stringing together
like a small chain of being
her life

but she resists
hieratic among teens, and I'm the groom
hearing little at the horse's ear
as they ride away
Nissaned, Volkswagened among themselves.

I tell you stuff, she said
and then you quarrel at me.
So I've learned, like an anthropologist
to say
and?

Poem Father

Defiant, desperate
despairing of an audience, I taped myself
and drunk at the finish
listened, triumphant
so exalted I forgot to take the tape out

which wouldn't matter
except that a week passed
and she sat cross-legged in front of the machine
cassettes scattered at her knees, and my voice, me–
huddled, dark, lugubrious–
filling the room.

God, Dad, what is this creepy stuff?
she asked, shuddering.
It's my poetry, dammit, I answered.
Oh, sorry, she said. *Can I tape over it?*
I borrowed the Sex Pistols and the Violent Femmes.

Sunbathing

Jansen ad
grease hot Hawaiian Tropic
coconut slick oil
flies hose gnats
lounge in her flesh, striped Wal-Mart
for the brown blond, nothing touched
for the sterile brown
my daughter striving, legs shaved
underarms
God, Dad, I'm so hairy!
sweat hot, suffering
bleached lip-hair, stark blond
pale wheat, drape shouldered
mask-face Kabuki
archaic Minoan
Nefertiti.

Sorry, My Mistake

Like finding shortness of breath
the key in the door on familiar emptiness
personal as charm, as home style
as mausoleums more mortal than granite
sofa, rug, lamps, VCR, TV
depressing as *Time* on the coffee table
mannequins of fantasy in the chairs

and I hear, moist as frogs, ferns, log-moss
moaning and gasps from the bathroom—
poor child, the flu, vague female
dangling as swamps, body laden
brilliant as her mind is
beyond pale-humid, frond-fecund–
the female, the daughter in my house

a forearm on the toilet bowl
her moist face dangling–
poor child
and me imagining ancient death, plague wailing
feverish as she dies in my arms.
Let me get you a cloth.
I'll wet it.
You want to go to the emergency room?

No, Dad.
Please, just go to bed.
And bourbon, acres of corn
the distilleries, it seemed
breathed at me.

I Forgot That

I asked to read her journal for English class.
It's the sort of thing parents do
show some interest
and she wrote pretty well except for the *Sooo's–*
Sooo pooped, *Sooo* p.o.'d, *Sooo* happy–
but that was a minor thing
her being a teenager

charming
more like a diary than a journal
until I came across
My Dad teaches college.
He didn't marry again and seems really sad
a lot of the time
and he hates grading papers.

Jesus.
She made me sound like a melancholy, miserable creep.
I felt flat, two-dimensional
to be mentioned in two sentences
stereotyped by a child
my own daughter.

It hurt my feelings
that kind of truth
and I told her.
Damn, Dad, I forgot that was in there
she said.

Driving Lessons

I've been on the driver's side for thirty years
and now, victimized, I cower behind the seat belt
clutching the dash, my right leg paralyzing the floor.
God, Dad, will you chill out!
Try to understand, I said.
It's not your driving.

I want to say
what little grip I had on the world
steering my destiny, is lost with you, over there
and I'm skittering like a shopping cart in the street
a baby carriage, a wheelchair
so for god's sake learn to drive

safe but quick
and I'll buy you a Nissan
a birthday present, a coming of age
so I can sit behind my own worry in the truck
my own menace.

Genteel Dad

She helps serve–
in the soft light, among linen and candles–
the wine, salad, beef at my dinner parties
and talks well enough with the guests
the chatter of *Rolling Stone, Newsweek, Natural History*
all of us contemporary as the evening news.

I glance at the phoenix, the acanthus in the wood
my Victorian oak, wondering if it's worse–
my buffet, corner cabinet, lion paws table, the scrolls on
          the chair-backs–
worse than the towers, black glass and steel, abstract as
          byte money
the strained faces at the screens, the white work
and always the street fear down below
buffeted, anxious as strangers.

I am nostalgic, doing for my friends, my daughter
what is part authentic, half made-up
remembrances of linen, china–so many spoons and forks!–
my dinner parties, artificed at with coffee and liqueur
stilted but comforting nonetheless
as we struggle with our teacups
to confound death.

IV

The Confession

No, she said
as if it didn't matter much
I'm not a virgin.
I was transported from my chair
gasp-hurled in silence to the same chair
same kitchen, same daughter

but I was altered
as by escape velocity made old
fate-fatigued, circumspect in an alien world
where she was the stranger, now, the other sex.
I felt ancient, ambassadorial, galaxy-weary.
Does he wear condoms? I asked.

Of course! she cried.
He doesn't want any trouble.
Not that he cares
and idiot me keeps going back.
I'm acting like a slut.
I know that.

I ached at her admission
as though, observing a nameless planet near a star
so vivid, so blue a place of acknowledgement and desire
that I was startled to see it was my own
that I beheld my earth, my home
as she wept.

Ancestors

No one wants false lights
reversed images, stage properties on a black screen
part film, part play to dream in
dead to consciousness
and with a shadowy immortality act out our scenes–

strange child, strange gods in a house
actors and audience all at once on the dusky stage
which is a hill
where mothers and fathers stand
mute witnesses

and when we rise, miraculous
the flights are a hideous ecstasy
as our arms brush tree limbs
stanchions, high-voltage wires, the cliffs
and we fall to the rocky stream.

Helpless before ancestors, so we dream.
We writhe in the bedsheets. We moan in the glittering dark
waking from immortal silhouettes, from shadows
suddenly into consciousness
shocked by the whereabouts in which we die.

Gaea's Children

for Charles, Gabriel and Helen

Our mother gives to her children unequal benefits.
Thoughtless in her love, she dotes on one
pets till the clay is rose fresh, stallion strong
yet one whose heart is a stone
smoothed in the stream of her caress
and heedless as her babbling to him
the smile of the water glitter.

Though with another, to make amends
she speaks as if the autumn were in her voice
pensive with wisdom, till the clay
like stunted laurel on a ridge
knows when to smile, when to sigh
and has a heart like the twig and leaf
bare to the sun and rain, grief and laughter.

And then, to right herself
sun warm and tender as the moon
she sings at dawn, and preens
like mockingbirds in the pear tree
and creates clay, April perfect
dancing and singing
yet with a kind and gentle heart, also
and wise as the petal fall in the wind.

Bird Sonnet

If patience were enough, I told my child
who came from her boyfriend's story, tear-wet
enough solicitude, compassion, tenderness
then what a passionate tree were yours, though blossom-mild
but your passion, too, will flutter beyond forbearance.
It will flit in the petaled wind
wild, wild for a palm to settle in
and there transformed–clawy hands and beak–
it will ease for a while your restless will
make you joyful, requite your dreams
and when the hand clinches, or drops
or rises in an arc, farewell
you'll adjust your throat, and with a human tongue
explain to him the inexplicable song.

Genesis II

I told my child a story
to ease the pain of love–
it was about the first pair
like mourning doves, and the man said:

When God turned away
it was a father, although a boy
and shirtless, out of the sun
who cradled me at his chest
and I was infant white, and cool
and soft as balm against his burning skin
bright bronze, and when he leaned
I drifted from his hands into the crib
and when he turned
he took my golden rib away
and I was left with a dark breastbone
and am bereft, as in a desert.

And I, she whispered:
curved near my heart is an eclipse
much brighter than the crescent moon
yet over the earth, whatever I see is dimmed
by the dark burning within–
the glittering arc at my breastbone
gold scimitar among the rest
was laid between me and her breasts
the girl's, my mother's breasts
like softest sand, the whitest shells
and the surging ocean.

Tuition Costs

I'd raised a child, practically
as if the end were something I'd thought about
prepared for, worked toward
when, in fact, I was amazed how little time was left
what with the ACT, SAT, the mailbox cluttered with
        college ads

loan forms, tuition costs, room and board
as if I were packaging her, fully insured
for Berkeley, Davis, somewhere deliverable to
and tampered with, probably
opened like a certified intelligence.

I'd raised a child
as if a million million hadn't done the same
yet it was fresh to me, fragrant as irises
as the climbing rose on the back porch
where I kept busy to distract myself

sawing fretwork, attaching it to the posts
and painting everything white, white as the roses
wonderfully unreal, a dream-labor
old fashioned as the moon in May, delicate
as she readied to go away.

Her Grandparents

When we visit in California
my parents nag *You've spoiled her rotten.*
But what do they know
who were too many pups at a dish
what love is
not to fight over
battle at

who see her freedom, her fearlessness
as license
when she hugs them
and goes her way
not to bicker
not to growl, or snarl
among them.

Ox in a Truck

When she leaves
what will I do
doom desolate–
so duty-done, will I die?
This change so sudden
like a sodden dam

the pile of earth which broke–
mud-water to the windows
the porch askew, the fence-debris
the child snagged by a post, boat-rescued
and what I had longed for as a father
now through

floundering in the yard
truck-muddy ox
I ask myself, free of my yoke-lease
what will I do, this aching aftermath
not lonely so much
as meaningless.

Letting Go

A father
like an open palm, sun-sieve as I
fleshy with fingers, the unclenching happiness
palm fountain like a stream, would wish

and you aglitter, sands diamonds
daughter, sift
the tickle-scratch
copper flutter and gone

its flitter dance over the mallows
the pollen swirl, etched gold-smear
leaf, water birch
its tiny turning and sailing-drift

dipping in the water babble–
so force-free
so like a father's love
I have wanted to be.

To Helen

at Berkeley

So young
too hurried but for a sigh
while I gaze, yearned out
at the flickers of wind-leaf across the lawn

and have seen, repeated
the damp-snow angel sleep
the wisp-white on the oak limbs
and the elm in the winter wind

shattering ice in the glittering sunlight
and crocuses in the slushy grass
crooked twigs, blossoms, leaf-unfurl–
but the hue rustlings, now

wine, gamboge, brown ease
press at the music of what I am
like fingertips calloused on strings
a claw hand, fret-slide

whirl-leaf, plucked strings
commensurate with the tumble-breeze
the autumn and the sweet despair
in the colored air.

Daughter Poem

For my own
for far death, feather
so gray lovely, tipped with white
and tiny in the weeds field
quill in the curl leaf of asters, goldenrod
little witness of flight

and you
while I memory-live, chestnut rich
etched yellow and blue pale, dry cool
the last sun on the south warm
face-furrow, I sigh and stretch

pointing sweet you, all east dew
and I, right west, write of you, a gauche
you, dawn hurry, all awkward flurry
my love
my daughter future in eagle
and small birds that sing.

Not Only Daughter

Routine lecture real
the authority burden carry
idol myself on a hill
Lear on my back
habit juggler, babbler of the civilized
I am not that
that obituary
only

or the coffee and mints while the cups crack
chitchat Van Buren Stonewall
talk talk parlor Eisenhower Truman
change and the same
while beyond us, father-uncle medals braid stars
coverts us
despair image borderless
death drift and Omega fire O nothing

but leaf-left
forfeit of parent-habit I
desperate as the hands weather
pitted-marble, wood-wormed as they clasp
as in askless prayer bow down and altar empty
death phrases
praise leaves brilliant and falling.